The MAILBOX®

CLASSROOM MANAGEMENT

PreK-K

SUPER SIMPLE!

W9-AWQ-797

Quick Tips and Timesaving Reproducibles for the Whole Year

- Classroom setup
- Routines and procedures
- Positive discipline
- Health and hygiene
- Organizing paperwork
- Parent conferences
- Circle-time management
- Smooth transitions
- Center-time management
- and MORE!

Over 160 management tools to choose from!

Managing Editor: Kelly Robertson

Editorial Team: Stephanie Affinito, Becky S. Andrews, Randi Austin, Diane Badden, Amber Barbee, Tonya Bays, Amy Brinton, Kimberley Bruck, Karen A. Brudnak, Kimberly Brugger-Murphy, Marie E. Cecchini, Clare Cox, Pam Crane, Jaime Cunningham, Kathryn Davenport, Roxanne LaBell Dearman, Beth Deki, Angela Fletcher, Pierce Foster, Susan Foulks, Deborah Garmon, Teresa Gibson, Karen Guess, Tazmen Hansen, Trystajill Harns, Erica Haver, Marsha Heim, Lori Z. Henry, Laura Johnson, Debra Liverman, Sharon Lorber, Kitty Lowrance, Coramarie Marinan, Brenda Miner, Amanda Monday, Suzanne Moore, Lisa Mountcasel, Jennifer Nunn, Mary Patton, Tina Petersen, Gerri Primak, Mark Rainey, Heather Reeder, Greg D. Rieves, Larissa Robinson, Mary Robles, Hope Rodgers, Amy Rodriguez, Deborah Ryan, Eliseo De Jesus Santos III, Rebecca Saunders, Kelly Smith, Donna K. Teal, Jill Tittsworth, Rachael Traylor, Sharon M. Tresino, Christine Vohs, Carole Watkins, Zane Williard, Virginia Zeletzki

www.themailbox.com

©2010 The Mailbox® Books
All rights reserved.
ISBN10 #1-56234-925-2 • ISBN13 #978-1-56234-925-7

Printed in the United States
10 9 8 7 6 5 4 3 2 1

HPS 211911

What's Inside

PRACTICAL tips for successful classroom management

Check out an "Editor's Pick" when you need an idea in a hurry!

Routines and Procedures

Editor's Pick

Restroom Request
Display a copy of the poster from page 16. Teach youngsters how to sign the word *bathroom* using American Sign Language, as shown. To limit classroom interruptions, have students perform the sign to request a bathroom break.

Bathroom

Lineup Lyrics
As students line up to leave the classroom, lead them in quietly singing the song shown. By the time youngsters sing the last line, they'll be ready to walk down the hall.

(sung to the tune of "The Wheels on the Bus")

In line my arms are by my side,
By my side, by my side.
In line my arms are by my side
All through the halls.

Continue with the following:
In line my feet are very quiet.
In line my eyes look straight ahead.

Clean and Tidy
Use a puppet with personality for a fun way to announce cleanup time. Motivate youngsters to get the classroom clean and tidy by walking the puppet to each center and reciting the poem shown.

Cleanup time comes after play.
We all must help put toys away.
On the shelf, place storybooks.
Put dress-up clothes back on the hooks.
The wooden blocks go in their case.
Let's take our time; it's not a race.
When the room is clean and neat,
Please tiptoe back to your seat.

See page 15 for a checklist of routines and procedures.

14   *Super Simple Classroom Management • ©The Mailbox® Books • TEC61255*

TIMESAVING assessments, checklists, patterns, and more

Name _____   Dates _____

Colors

red	green	orange	brown	yellow	purple	blue	black

Shapes and Solids

Number Sense

	0	1	2	3	4	5	6	7	8	9	10	11	12	13	14	15	16	17	18	19	20	21	22	23	24	25	26	27	28	29	30
Recognizes Numbers																															
Creates Sets																															
Writes Numbers																															

Letters

	A	B	C	D	E	F	G	H	I	J	K	L	M	N	O	P	Q	R	S	T	U	V	W	X	Y	Z
Recognizes Uppercase Letters																										
Recognizes Lowercase Letters																										
Produces Sound(s)																										

Notes:

Super Simple Classroom Management • ©The Mailbox® Books • TEC61255

Note to the teacher: Use with "Grab-and-Go Assessment" on page 33.

Name _____

Centers

Center		Finishe
Literacy	A B C	
Writing		
Math	1 2 3	
Art		
Science		
Block		
Dramatic Play		
Fine Motor		

Super Simple Classroom Management • ©The Mailbox® Books • TEC61255

50   **Note to the teacher:** Give each child a copy of the page and have him draw a smiley face in the appropriate box by each visit.

Reminder Patterns
Use with "Stop and Check" on page 93.

STOP
Please check this folder for an important note.
TEC61255

STOP
Please check this folder for an important note.
TEC61255

STOP
Please check this folder for an important note.
TEC61255

STOP
Please check this folder for an important note.
TEC61255

94   *Super Simple Classroom Management • ©The Mailbox® Books • TEC61255*

Reproducible forms and notes you can **CUSTOMIZE** online

Field Trip Log

Name of location:
Address:
Phone number:
Contact person:
Cost per child: _____ Per adult:
Bag lunch or snack: ☐ yes ☐ no
Chaperones:

Theme-related trip? ☐ yes ☐ no
If yes, name of theme:
Would you take this trip again? ☐ yes ☐ no
Comments:

71

Note to the teacher: Use with "Tracking Trips" on page 70.

"Dino-mite" News From School

_____ had a great day because _____

teacher's signature

Dear Family,
Please help _____ with _____.
Some suggestions are:

Thank you for your help.

teacher's signature

Look for this symbol!

Welcome to Open House!

Room _____

teacher's name

Cover Your Mouth When You Cough or Sneeze, Please!

Achoo!

Full-color tools that you simply **PULL OUT AND USE**

Super Simple Classroom Management • ©The Mailbox® Books • TEC61255   3

Table of Contents

Before the First Day

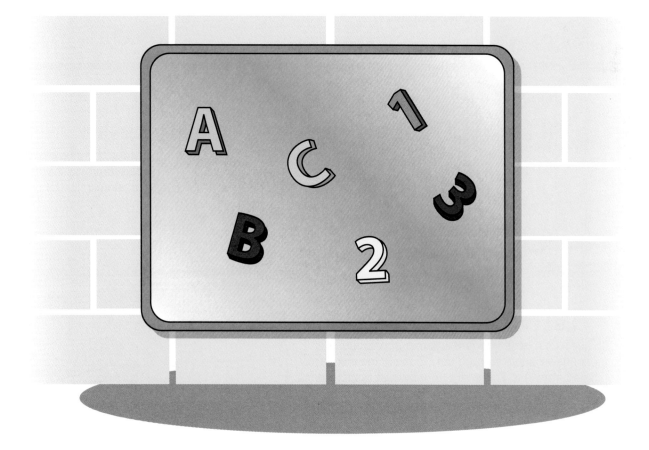

Bulletin Boards and Displays

Getting to Know You

Before the start of school, mail each student a copy of the cutout on page 7 along with a note asking parents to help their child decorate the cutout so it looks like herself. On the first day of school, have each child share her cutout and something about herself with the class. Then display the completed projects on a bulletin board.

Shining Stars

Cover a class supply of tagboard stars with aluminum foil. On the first day of school, take a photo of each child. Attach each photo to a star; then display the stars on a board covered with dark paper. Showcase each youngster's best work by attaching it to the board with his personalized star.

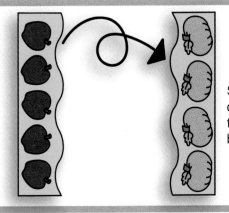

Back-to-Back Borders

Save time changing bulletin board borders by gluing two different borders back-to-back and then trimming them to fit. When you're ready for a change, simply flip the border over to display the new design.

Letters at Your Fingertips

To keep your bulletin board letters organized, use an inexpensive photo storage box. Place in the box cards labeled from A to Z; then file your bulletin board letters behind the appropriate dividers. Put small pieces, such as punctuation marks, in a resealable plastic bag and store them in the box as well.

TEC61255

Editor's Pick

Relaxation Station

To provide a space for a child who needs some time to calm down, arrange a quiet area with comfortable seating, such as a beanbag chair or large floor pillows. Include a cuddly stuffed animal to comfort the child and a variety of stress balls to help him release tension.

Noisy or Quiet?

When deciding where to place your centers, keep in mind the noise that busy youngsters may produce in each area and how it may affect the learning of others. Separate noisy areas, such as the block center and dramatic-play area, from quiet areas, such as the writing center and reading area.

The Perfect Setup

As you set up your classroom, arrange bookcases and furniture so they divide the room into defined learning areas. Be sure the arrangement provides clear pathways for walking, offers a view of youngsters working in each center, and limits open areas that encourage running.

See page 9 for a list of center ideas and page 10 for classroom labels.

Super Classroom Centers

Check out this handy list of classroom centers and suggested supplies to place in each one.

- **Blocks:** assorted blocks; LEGO toys; toy animals, people, vehicles, and road signs; old blueprints; plastic tools; hard hats

- **Art:** assorted paper for painting and drawing, easel, watercolors, play dough with tools, craft tape, safety scissors, collage materials, glue

- **Games:** puzzles, pattern blocks, interlocking toys, stringing beads, lacing cards, dressing frames, Geoboards, magnetic letters and numbers, lotto games, board games, card games

- **Reading:** variety of children's books, big books, books with tapes, tape player, headphones, puppets, flannelboard, cozy furniture

- **Writing:** markers, crayons, pencils, chalk, chalkboards, assorted paper, tracing templates, scissors, tape, envelopes, small staplers, alphabet strip

- **Sensory:** sensory table or large plastic tubs, water, sand, potting soil, measuring cups, scoops, funnels, sifters, small plastic rakes and shovels, sponges, eyedroppers, turkey basters

- **Science:** magnifying glasses, balance scale, tape measures, magnets, tweezers, tongs, nontoxic plants, collections to explore (shells, rocks, leaves)

- **Dramatic Play:** dress-up clothes and accessories, dishware, utensils, empty food boxes, plastic food, telephones with the cords removed, phone books, recipe books, dolls

Try these unique dramatic-play settings!

- Farmer's Market
- Post Office
- Flower Shop
- Gift Shop
- Shoe Store
- Restaurant
- Doctor's Office
- Veterinarian's Office
- Hair Salon

TEC61255

TEC61255

TEC61255

TEC61255

TEC61255

TEC61255

Editor's Pick

Working on the Wall

To create a space-saving work area, attach a metal cookie tray to the lower portion of a wall using double-sided tape. Then place magnetic manipulatives, such as letters or numbers, on the tray.

Theme Boxes

Gather an empty cardboard or plastic box with a lid for each theme you teach. Label the outside of each box with the name of a unit. Then place inside the box a copy of the lesson plans and materials—such as books, games, and props—that correlate with each unit. The boxes can be neatly stacked and stored until needed.

Color Coded

Collect empty cereal boxes to store construction paper. Cut off the top flaps and cover each box with a different color of construction paper. Then place the corresponding colored paper and scraps in each box. Store the boxes within children's reach.

Red

See page 12 for a list of ways to maximize your classroom space using recycled items.

Simple Storage Solutions

Here's a list of handy storage items made by reusing or recycling materials.

- **Plastic zippered bedding or curtain bag:** store games, toys, and manipulatives

- **Magnetic photo album:** store window clings under the adhesive pages

- **Nylon laundry bag:** store and carry playground equipment

- **Cardboard drink holder from fast-food restaurant:** paint-cup holder

- **Large, clear plastic jar with lid:** store art supplies, such as pom-poms, cotton balls, and paintbrushes

- **Clean pillowcase:** store bedding for rest time

- **Gallon-size ice cream bucket with handle:** store materials such as pattern blocks, toy animals, and people figurines

- **Lidded frosting container:** store rolled-up bulletin board border

- **Baby wipe box:** store stickers or flannelboard pieces

- **Cardboard tube:** store rolled-up charts and posters

See page 13 for a form to use to ask for donations of materials.

Calling All Parents!

Our class needs your help! Please send any of these items. We will make good use of them in our classroom. Thanks!

Sincerely,

_____
teacher

_____   _____

_____   _____

_____   _____

_____   _____

Calling All Parents!

Our class needs your help! Please send any of these items. We will make good use of them in our classroom. Thanks!

Sincerely,

_____
teacher

_____   _____

_____   _____

_____   _____

_____   _____

Note to the teacher: Use this form to help collect the supplies from page 12.

Routines and Procedures

Restroom Request

Display a copy of the poster from page 16. Teach youngsters how to sign the word *bathroom* using American Sign Language, as shown. To limit classroom interruptions, have students perform the sign to request a bathroom break.

Bathroom

Lineup Lyrics

As students line up to leave the classroom, lead them in quietly singing the song shown. By the time youngsters sing the last line, they'll be ready to walk down the hall.

(sung to the tune of "The Wheels on the Bus")

In line my arms are by my side,
By my side, by my side.
In line my arms are by my side
All through the halls.

Continue with the following:
In line my feet are very quiet.
In line my eyes look straight ahead.

Clean and Tidy

Use a puppet with personality for a fun way to announce cleanup time. Motivate youngsters to get the classroom clean and tidy by walking the puppet to each center and reciting the poem shown.

Cleanup time comes after play.
We all must help put toys away.
On the shelf, place storybooks.
Put dress-up clothes back on the hooks.
The wooden blocks go in their case.
Let's take our time; it's not a race.
When the room is clean and neat,
Please tiptoe back to your seat.

See page 15 for a checklist of routines and procedures.

Establish Your Classroom Procedures

Check the procedures you want to teach your new class.

☐ Entering the classroom

☐ Hanging up coats and bookbags

☐ Starting the day

☐ Lining up

☐ Fire drill procedure

☐ Walking in the hallway

☐ Lunchtime procedure

☐ When and how to use the restroom

☐ What to do if you need help

☐ Asking questions

☐ When and how to use the water fountain

☐ When and how to use the sink

☐ Ending the day

☐ Getting toys, books, and supplies

☐ Putting away toys, books, and supplies

☐ Working at a center

☐ Circle-time procedure

☐ Snacktime procedure

☐ Naptime procedure

☐ Getting ready for outdoor play

☐ Outdoor play

☐ Indoor play

☐ Throwing away trash

☐ What to do with unfinished work

☐ Getting a tissue

☐ Playing with the class pet

☐ Feeding the class pet

☐ Other: _____

☐ Other: _____

☐ Other: _____

TIPS-4-U

✓ For each procedure checked, list two to four steps you want students to follow.

✓ Add stars by the procedures you want to teach first.

✓ Practice each procedure with students.

Bathroom

Super Simple Classroom Management • ©The Mailbox® Books • TEC61255

16   **Note to the teacher:** Use with "Restroom Request" on page 14.

At the Beginning of the Year

Our Community Rules

Talk quietly.

Look at the teacher.

Listen to instructions.

Keep your hands to yourself.

Walk when inside.

The First Day

Editor's Pick

Handy Exchanges

Read aloud *The Kissing Hand* by Audrey Penn. After discussing the story, invite youngsters to share how they feel about being away from their families and how they think their families feel about being away from them. Next, have each child trace her hand and cut out the tracing; then attach a heart sticker to the cutout. Send home the materials needed for each parent to do the same. Then have youngsters and parents exchange their kissing hands.

First-Day Fears

Help little ones feel more comfortable on the first day of school by placing a batch of play dough and play dough tools at each of several different tables. Invite parents to spend a few minutes squishing and pounding the dough with their children. The active engagement and physical activity will help ease youngsters' first-day jitters.

All About You!

Place in a tote bag several items that reveal things about you, such as photos of your family or pets, a picture of your favorite food, and a hobby-related item. In turn, invite volunteers to each remove an item from the bag. Share the significance of the item as students pass it around to take a closer look. Invite youngsters to ask questions to help them become more familiar and comfortable with you.

All Aboard!

Pretend to be a train conductor and give each child a mock train ticket. Have students pretend to board a train as they line up behind you. Start the train engine by saying, "Toot! Toot!" Then lead youngsters on a train ride around the room and point out important places, such as the learning centers, the bathroom, the sink, and the trash can.

Train Ticket

Establishing Class Rules

Picture-Perfect Behavior

Provide youngsters with a visual reminder of your classroom rules. Take photographs of students demonstrating positive behaviors as they follow the rules. Mount each photo on a sheet of tagboard; then label each photo with its matching rule. Post the reminders on a wall.

Use walking feet.

Put your toys away.

Act It Out

After introducing your class rules, announce a rule, such as "Use an indoor voice." Then perform the opposite of the rule by exaggerating inappropriate behaviors, such as yelling across the room or talking very loudly. Discuss why those behaviors are inappropriate; then guide students to demonstrate appropriate ways to follow the rule.

Puppet Pals

Invite your youngsters to help you create classroom rules in a fun, interactive way. Enlist the help of two puppets to role-play scenarios that display both positive and negative behaviors. Use the playful scenarios to guide youngsters in developing appropriate classroom rules.

It's in the Bag

Write several classroom rules on separate strips of paper. Do the same for several statements that would not be rules, such as "Always leave your trash on the table" or "Never put toys away when you're finished playing." In turn, pull each strip of paper from the bag and read it aloud. Then encourage youngsters to discuss which statements would make appropriate classroom rules and which ones would not.

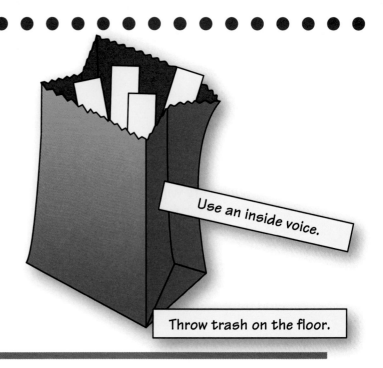

Use an inside voice.

Throw trash on the floor.

Sign Here!

Work together with your students to create a classroom constitution. Discuss several scenarios involving classroom behavior. Ask youngsters about the appropriate behavior for each situation, leading them to develop classroom rules. Once the rules have been established, list them on a large sheet of paper and have each youngster sign his name. Then post the resulting classroom constitution on a wall.

Follow the Rules

Cut out a copy of the cards on page 21 and mount them on a poster board schoolhouse cutout like the one shown. In turn, have students identify each picture; then lead them in brainstorming a classroom rule related to the pictured body part. For example, for the feet, guide youngsters to develop a rule that involves walking inside. Record each rule beside the corresponding picture.

Our Community Rules

Talk quietly.

Look at the teacher.

Listen to instructions.

Keep your hands to yourself.

Walk when inside.

Use with "Follow the Rules" on page 20.

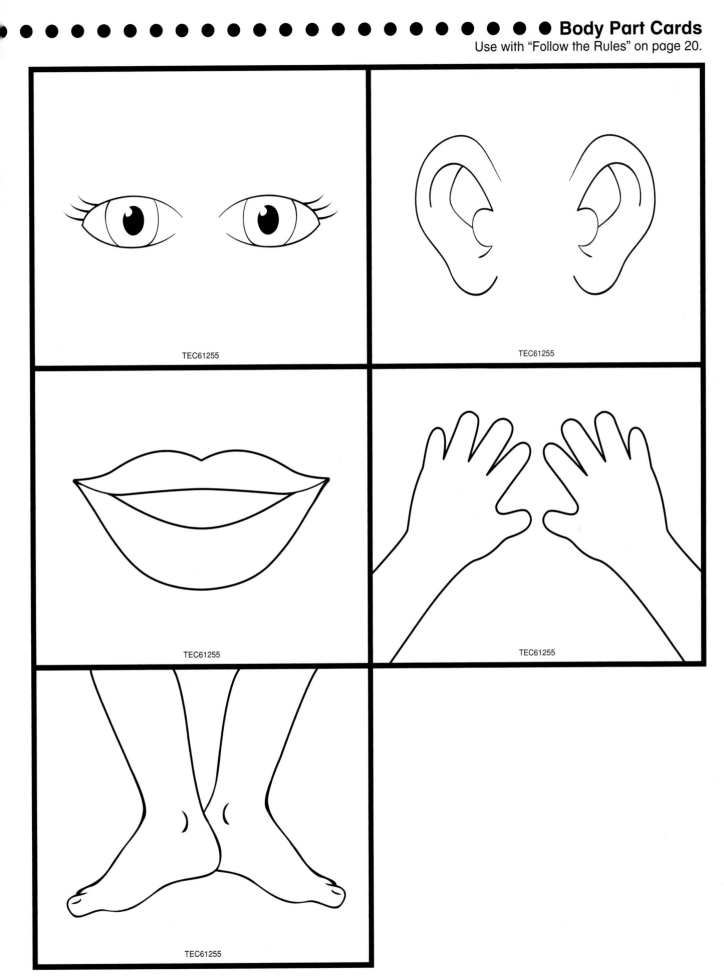

TEC61255

TEC61255

TEC61255

TEC61255

TEC61255

Open House

Open House Slideshow

If your open house takes place after the school year begins, take photos of students at work and play. Use the pictures to create a slideshow on your computer screensaver; then place the computer in a central location for parents to view. If desired, take photos of parents during the visit and then present a slideshow of the parents to your students!

Center Time for Parents

Prior to open house, set up your centers. When parents arrive, provide them with a list of the skills practiced at each center. Invite parents to explore each center. Then lead parents in a discussion about the skill development that learning centers provide.

Merry Messages

Have each child draw a picture for his parents and then dictate a message for you to write on his drawing. Before open house, place each picture at a table along with a special treat for parents. During the visit, invite parents to respond to their children's messages. (Write a special note for each child whose parents were unable to attend.)Then leave the responses on the tables for youngsters to find the following day.

I love you.

Mark

My Favorites List

Help each child prepare a list of places and things she would like her parents to visit during open house, such as her favorite center, her cubby, her work on display, or a class pet. Have her parents place a sticker next to each item on her list after they have seen it.

I want you to see

my cubby ☆

my painting ☆

housekeeping ☆

the computer station

our pet gerbil

Teacher on Display

Open house is the perfect time to showcase not only your classroom but yourself as well. To help parents get to know you, create a display about yourself. For example, you might display family photos, special awards or certificates, or items relating to a hobby. A display like this is a great way to jump-start parent-teacher relationships.

Classroom Mural

If students are invited to your open house, plan a special project that will get them involved while parents browse the classroom and visit with staff. Attach a large sheet of white bulletin board paper to a wall and provide a container of large crayons. Then encourage visiting youngsters to create a cooperative mural.

See page 24 for open house invitations and page 25 for an open house welcome sign.

You're invited to open house!

Date: _____ Time: _____

Location: _____

Ring a bell!
Give a cheer!
We've begun
A new school year!

Hope to see you there!

Sincerely,

_____

You're invited to open house!

Date: _____ Time: _____

Location: _____

Ring a bell!
Give a cheer!
We've begun
A new school year!

Hope to see you there!

Sincerely,

_____

Welcome to Open House!

Room _____

_____
teacher's name

All Year Long

Aides and Volunteers

Editor's Pick

Always Ready

To prepare for volunteers, place two tubs labeled as shown in a designated location. Place in the tub labeled "For the Kids" review games, puzzles, manipulatives, or other activities a volunteer can do with students. Place in the tub labeled "For the Teacher" work such as papers to be graded or filed and laminated items to be cut out. When a volunteer arrives, simply direct her to choose a task from one of the boxes.

For the Kids

For the Teacher

Teamwork

Let your aide know the importance of the role she plays by setting aside time each week to chat about plans for the following week. Discuss lesson plans, skills to be covered, and information about special events. Be sure to share any lessons she'll be helping teach as well. Then encourage her to share ideas or ask questions about the plans.

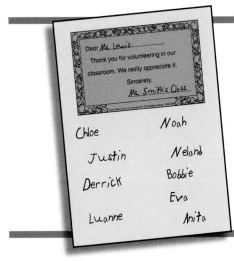

Dear _Ms. Lewis_
Thank you for volunteering in our classroom. We really appreciate it.
Sincerely,
Ms. Smith's Class

Chloe   Noah
Justin   Neland
Derrick   Bobbie
             Eva
Luanne   Anita

Simple Thanks

Here's a quick yet meaningful way to thank classroom volunteers. Attach a personalized copy of a thank-you note from page 29 to a sheet of construction paper. Then invite each youngster to write his name below the note.

Pick a Folder

To make it easy for volunteers to work with individual students, personalize a folder for each child. Place in each folder several activities for the youngster to complete; also include a list of the activities in his folder. Store the folders and any materials needed for the activities in a container. A volunteer chooses a folder, helps the child complete one of the activities, and then checks it off the list.

See page 30 for information cards to help you organize volunteers.

Dear _____,

Thank you for volunteering in our classroom. We really appreciate it.

Sincerely,

_____

Dear _____,

Thank you for volunteering in our classroom. We really appreciate it.

Sincerely,

_____

Volunteers Needed

If you are able to volunteer, please fill out this form and return it to school. Thanks in advance for your help.

Name: _____   Phone: _____

Email: _____

I can contribute by

☐ working with students   ☐ preparing materials at school

☐ chaperoning a field trip   ☐ supplying materials

☐ preparing materials at home   ☐ helping at special events

☐ Other_____

Super Simple Classroom Management • ©The Mailbox® Books • TEC61255

Volunteers Needed

If you are able to volunteer, please fill out this form and return it to school. Thanks in advance for your help.

Name: _____   Phone: _____

Email: _____

I can contribute by

☐ working with students   ☐ preparing materials at school

☐ chaperoning a field trip   ☐ supplying materials

☐ preparing materials at home   ☐ helping at special events

☐ Other_____

Super Simple Classroom Management • ©The Mailbox® Books • TEC61255

All About Tomorrow

Dismissal is a perfect time to get youngsters excited about the next school day. Title a small magnetic board as shown and make cards to represent the days of the week and the activities that occur regularly throughout the school year. Attach a magnet to the back of each card. Before dismissal, place on the board the cards pertaining to the next school day as you share this information with students.

What will we do on Friday?

Music   Special Visitor   Game Day

Morning Activities

Keep youngsters busy during arrival time with these fun-filled containers. Stock each of five containers with engaging materials, such as manipulatives, books, and puzzles. Divide students into five groups. During arrival time, direct each group to investigate the materials in a container. To keep student interest high, change the materials every few weeks.

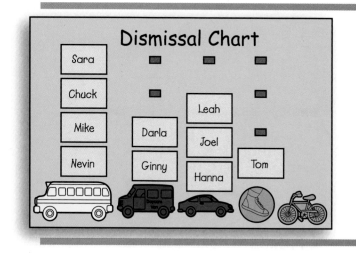

Dismissal Chart

Sara
Chuck
Mike
Nevin
Darla
Ginny
Leah
Joel
Hanna
Tom

Dismissal Chart

Color and cut out a copy of the patterns on page 32 and attach them to a chart like the one shown. Affix the loop side of Velcro fasteners in a column above each pattern. Then personalize a card for each student and attach the hook side of a Velcro fastener to the back. Have each child place his card above the image that represents his dismissal transportation. If a child's dismissal transportation changes, it's a snap to update the chart.

Tidy Up

Make afternoon cleanup quick and easy by enlisting students' help. Assign youngsters jobs, such as picking up trash, wiping tables, or stacking chairs. Giving little ones responsibilities encourages a sense of ownership and pride in their classroom and ensures the room will be neat following dismissal.

Transportation Patterns

Use with "Dismissal Chart" on page 31.

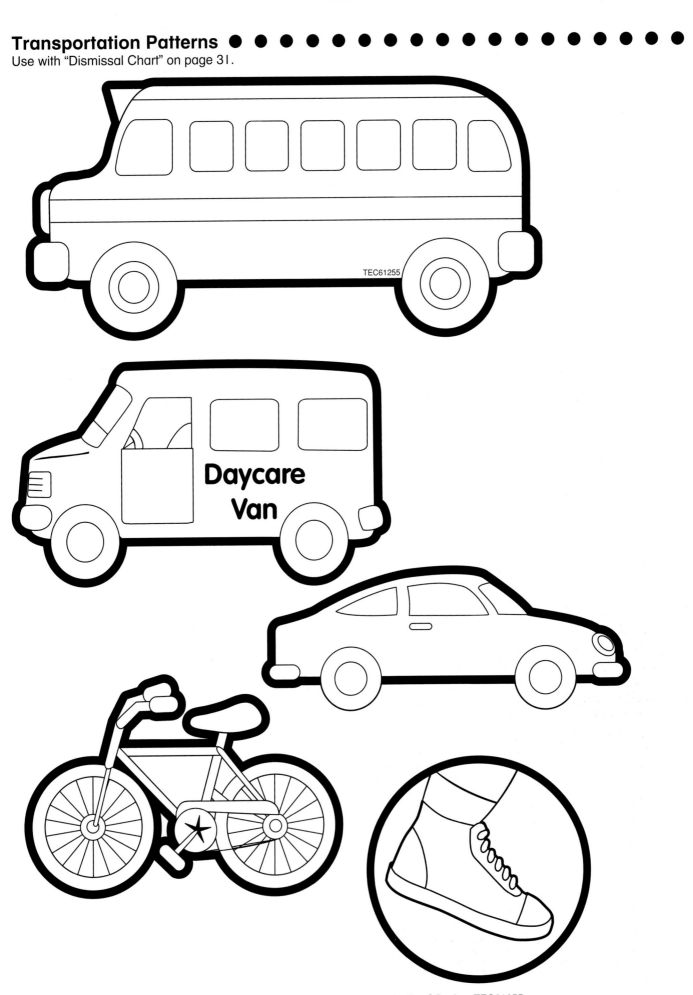

TEC61255

Daycare Van

Assessments

Editor's Pick

Snapshot Assessments

Photos of students engaged in classroom activities make a great informal assessment tool. When you notice a child doing something noteworthy, take a photo of him and jot a quick note and the date on a sticky note. Then attach the note to the back of the photo and place it in the student's file.

3/27/09

Jasper is measuring the length of the room with blocks.

Take Note

To easily keep anecdotal notes on students, make one or more copies of the observation log on page 34 and label each page with the current month. Each day choose a different child and write her name and the date in a section of the log. Throughout the day, observe the child in various situations and make brief notes.

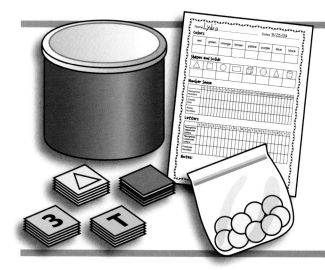

Grab-and-Go Assessment

For each student, personalize a copy of the assessment sheet on page 35 and place the copies in a binder. Gather a set of cards to match each skill on the assessment. Place the card sets in a container along with a supply of counters, the binder, and several pens of different colors. Throughout the year, assess the skills appropriate for each student and record the information on her sheet using a different-colored pen each time.

Get Moving

Try this tip to help youngsters awaken their brains before you give them an assessment. Write a simple movement on each of several slips of paper and place the slips in a small bag. Have a student take a slip from the bag. Read it to him and invite him to lead the class in performing the movement ten times.

Observation Log for _____

Name _____ Date _____	Name _____ Date _____	Name _____ Date _____
Name _____ Date _____	Name _____ Date _____	Name _____ Date _____
Name _____ Date _____	Name _____ Date _____	Name _____ Date _____
Name _____ Date _____	Name _____ Date _____	Name _____ Date _____
Name _____ Date _____	Name _____ Date _____	Name _____ Date _____

Super Simple Classroom Management • ©The Mailbox® Books • TEC61255

Name _____ Dates _____

Colors

red	green	orange	brown	yellow	purple	blue	black

Shapes and Solids

Number Sense

	0	1	2	3	4	5	6	7	8	9	10	11	12	13	14	15	16	17	18	19	20	21	22	23	24	25	26	27	28	29	30
Recognizes Numbers																															
Creates Sets																															
Writes Numbers																															

Letters

	A	B	C	D	E	F	G	H	I	J	K	L	M	N	O	P	Q	R	S	T	U	V	W	X	Y	Z
Recognizes Uppercase Letters																										
Recognizes Lowercase Letters																										
Produces Sound(s)																										

Notes:

A Present for Grandma

Books for Birthdays

Give students the gift of literacy! At the beginning of the school year, ask each family to donate an inexpensive or gently used book. Place these books in a container labeled "Birthday Books." On a child's birthday, invite her to select a book to take home as a gift to enjoy with her family.

Choose a Story

For an enjoyable way to celebrate a birthday, place several birthday-themed books in a decorated box. On a child's birthday have him choose a book from the box for you to read aloud to the class.

Birthday Wishes

When a birthday child arrives at school, give him a cake cutout (pattern on page 38). Have him decorate the cake and add paper candles to match his age. When he is satisfied with his work, invite each classmate to sign her name on the back of the cake.

Ready to Celebrate

To avoid missing a birthday, label a folder for each month of the school year. Inside each folder, place a prepared birthday card or badge for each student who has a birthday during that month. When a child's special day arrives, you'll be ready to celebrate.

Birthdays on Display

Prepare a bulletin board titled "Happy Birthday." Then take a photo of each student wearing a birthday hat or crown. Attach each child's photo to a piece of celebration-themed paper labeled with her birthdate. Then display the photos on the prepared board.

Small-Group Fun

To keep holidays and other special celebration days stress-free, set up a variety of celebration-themed stations instead of whole-group activities. Enlist parent volunteers to help at each station. Then divide students into small groups and have each group rotate among the stations.

A Special Gift

On a youngster's birthday, invite him to share items that are special to him. Decorate a lidded box as shown and attach to the inside of the lid a copy of the note at the top of page 39. Send the box home with a child a few days before his birthday. (Be sure to assign alternate dates for students whose birthdays fall when school is not in session.) When he returns the box to school on his birthday, invite him to share its contents with his classmates.

Photo Album

See the bottom of page 39 for a class celebration invitation and page 40 for a birthday card.

Birthday Cake Pattern

Use with "Birthday Wishes" on page 36.

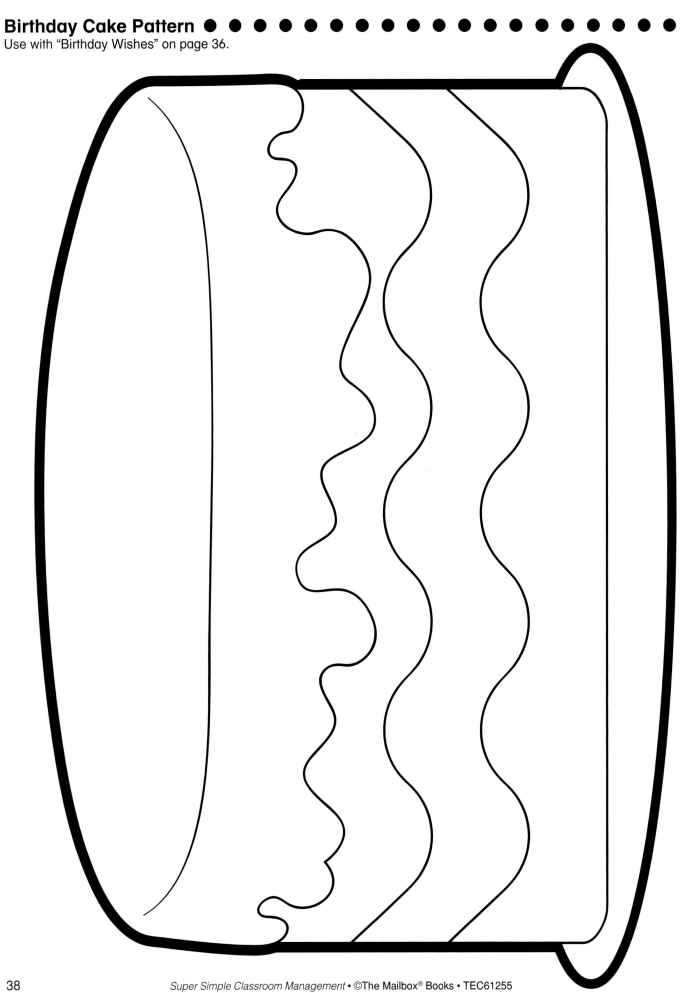

Dear Parent,

Please assist me in celebrating your child's birthday by helping him/her fill this box with small items that are special to him/her. Examples include photos, toys, and books. Have your child bring the filled box to school on his/her birthday. Thanks in advance for your help.

Sincerely,

_____
teacher

Super Simple Classroom Management • ©The Mailbox® Books • TEC61255

Note to the teacher: Use with "A Special Gift" on page 37.

Dear Parent/Guardian,

CELEBRATE!!

You are invited to _____
event

at our school on _____,
day

_____.
date

I hope to see you there.

Sincerely,

_____
teacher

Super Simple Classroom Management • ©The Mailbox® Books • TEC61255

Note to the teacher: Use the invitation to invite parents to join you during special events.

39

Happy Birthday to

_____

Note to the teacher: Personalize a copy of this page for a child on his birthday. Invite him to color the page as desired.

Editor's Pick

Counting Caterpillar

Add this adorable friend to your calendar to help youngsters keep track of the number of days they've been in school! Decorate a circle cutout so it resembles a caterpillar's head. Then post the cutout near your calendar area and place additional circle cutouts nearby. On the first day of school, write the number 1 on a cutout and have a child attach it next to the caterpillar's head. Continue adding a numbered cutout each school day until the end of the year. Youngsters will love to watch this caterpillar grow!

Sing the Months

To help youngsters remember the months of the year, encourage them to sing this simple little ditty!

(sung to the tune of "Ten Little Indians")

January, February, March, and April,
May, June, July, and August,
September, October, November, December—
These are the months of the year!

jumping

clapping

marching

nodding

Wiggles Be Gone!

Incorporate movement into your calendar time to keep restless wiggles at bay. Write the names of different actions on small cards. Then place the cards in a container. Each morning, have a child choose a card and help him read the action. Prompt students to repeat the action as they count to the current date.

The Envelope, Please

With this tip, your calendar time will be organized for the entire year. Place monthly calendar pieces in separate manila envelopes. Then attach the hook side of a Velcro fastener to each envelope. Attach the loop side of one fastener near your calendar and then attach the appropriate envelope. (Store the remaining envelopes until needed.) Now you have easy access to all the cutouts needed for calendar time!

Days of the Week

Help students remember the days of the week with this giggle-inducing idea! Encourage youngsters to recite the days of the week with you. Then prompt them to recite the days using a voice that's high-pitched. Continue having students repeat the days of the week with a variety of different voices, such as low-pitched, loud, quiet, and silly.

Pleasing Pointers

In advance, make several simple pointers by attaching craft foam cutouts, silk flowers, or finger puppets to separate dowel rods. Then store the pointers in a container. For each calendar-time session, ask a different child to choose a pointer and then use it to assist with calendar time.

See pages 43 and 45 for ready-to-go calendar pieces and page 47 for a reproducible calendar template.

TEC61255

TEC61255

TEC61255

TEC61255

TEC61255

TEC61255

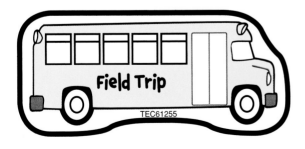

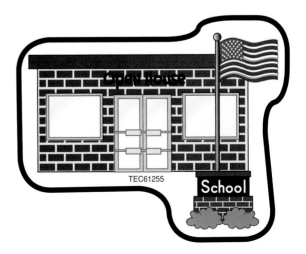

Sunday	Monday	Tuesday	Wednesday	Thursday	Friday	day

Super Simple Classroom Management • ©The Mailbox® Books • TEC61255

Note to the teacher: Copy this calendar and label it to correspond to the desired month. Add any appropriate information and then send home a copy with each youngster to alert families to upcoming events.

 Editor's Pick

Center Captains

Here's a way to promote student independence during center time. For each center, designate a child to be the captain and give her a construction paper badge to wear. Explain to youngsters that each captain is responsible for reminding the students at her center to work quietly and clean up at the end of the allotted time.

Center Captain

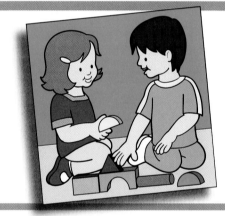

Take a Photo!

Before students visit your centers, walk them through each center and show them the items available and how to clean up. Then invite a few children to participate in each center to demonstrate what they learned. Take photographs of the youngsters. The next day, post the photos next to the appropriate centers. What a fun visual reminder of appropriate center-time behavior!

Marvelous Management

To have youngsters manage their own centers, place a clipboard with a laminated class list at each center along with a wipe-off marker. When a youngster completes the center task, he crosses his name off the list. Encourage youngsters to complete the task at each center by the end of the week.

Spiffy Cleanup

For extra easy center cleanup, take photographs of each center with everything put away appropriately. Then post the photos near the center. Youngsters clean up the centers and then consult the photos to make sure everything is in its proper place.

Center Clips

In advance, post a piece of tagboard in each center, making sure each piece is a different color. Decide how many students can comfortably work in each center. Then use paint or markers to make sets of coordinating-color clothespins. Clip each set of clothespins to the appropriate tagboard piece. To visit a center, a child removes a clothespin and attaches it to his shirt. If all the clothespins are taken, he knows that center is full.

Center Inspector

Each day designate a child to be the center inspector and give her a large plastic magnifying glass. When students are finished cleaning up after center time, the center inspector goes from center to center with the magnifying glass in hand, making sure the areas are neat and tidy.

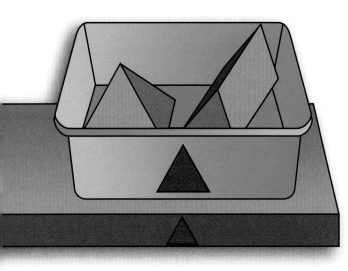

Center Tubs

These portable centers are perfect for classrooms with limited space! Simply place the items for individual centers in separate tubs. Label the tubs with different shape cutouts. Then label the shelf where each center is stored with the matching shape. A youngster takes a tub to a workspace and then returns it to the appropriate shelf when he is finished.

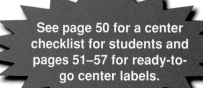

See page 50 for a center checklist for students and pages 51–57 for ready-to-go center labels.

Centers

Center		Finished
Literacy	A B C	
Writing		
Math	1 2 3	
Art		
Science		
Block		
Dramatic Play		
Fine Motor		

Note to the teacher: Give each child a copy of the page and have him draw a smiley face in the appropriate box by each center he visits.

Literacy Center

Writing Center

TEC61255

Math Center

Art Center

Science Center

Block Center

Dramatic-Play
Area

Fine-Motor
Area

TEC61255

TEC61255

58

Circle Time

Ready-to-Go Basket

To prepare for a successful circle time, put together a basket containing the things you need, such as books, song cards, transition-time activities, reminder notes, props, or materials. Place the basket in your group-time area, and you're ready to go!

Energy Release

Engage little ones in this movement activity to help them release excess energy before circle time. Or try it during circle time if youngsters need to get the wiggles out!

Raise my eyebrows,
Wiggle my nose,
Shrug my shoulders,
Wiggle my toes,
Snap my fingers,
Clap, clap, clap!
Then fold my hands on my lap.

Busy Hands

Help keep little hands busy during circle time. Keep a supply of small squishy balls or beanbags on hand. If a youngster demonstrates a need to use his hands, give him one of the objects to quietly manipulate. The sensory stimulation will keep his hands busy in a positive way.

Talking Stick

Help youngsters understand there is a time to talk and a time to listen. Attach a die-cut shape to the top of a paint stir stick; then decorate the prop with craft materials. Explain to youngsters that the person holding the talking stick is the one who speaks while everyone else listens. Then, in turn, pass the prop to each student and have youngsters practice listening and speaking.

Sit-Upons

For each child, label a different large tagboard shape with her name. Attach the hook side of a Velcro fastener to the back of each shape. Position the shapes on the floor to give each child her personal space. The Velcro fastener not only secures the shapes to the carpet but also makes it easy to rearrange them.

Strategic Seating

To keep youngsters who distract each other separated and to help students know where to sit, try this. Make a large masking tape outline on the floor in your group-time area and use a permanent marker to write each child's name along the outline. Should the seating arrangement need to be changed, simply remove the outline and make a new one.

Aisha   Kirin   Juan   Lauren   Claire   Luis   Alison   Jada   Amber   Maria

Classroom Community

Community Spirit

Enlarge a class photo and mount it on a sheet of tagboard. Puzzle-cut the photo into 12 pieces; then trace each piece onto a second sheet of tagboard to make a puzzle base. Each time a student displays community-minded behavior, discuss the act with the class; then have the child glue a puzzle piece to the matching outline on the base. After the puzzle is complete, hang it on a wall or door with the title "Our Class Has Community Spirit!"

Catching Kindness

Build a caring classroom as you create a kindness chain. When you see a child performing an act of kindness, write on a paper strip her name and what you observed her doing. Staple the strip to make a loop and share it with the class. Tell what you observed and praise the child for her kind deed. Continue in the same manner for each act of kindness you observe, attaching each new link to make a chain.

Classroom Star

Before dismissal, lead an informal chat to recap the day's events. Ask each child to name something positive he did, such as helping to clean up, sharing his toys, using kind words, or comforting a classmate who was sad. After he shares, praise his efforts and have him attach a star sticker to a large star cutout. Once the star is filled with stickers, reward the class with a special privilege or treat.

Classroom Jobs

Cubby Keeper

To help keep cubbies neat, assign the job of cubby keeper. Attach a card like the one shown to each child's cubby. Have the cubby keeper check each cubby a few times a day, such as after arrival and after rest time and then remind his classmates to tidy up their cubbies, if needed. At the end of the day, place a small sticker on each card attached to a tidy cubby.

Say and Go

Add the job of skill holder to your classroom job list. Program a blank card with a picture, a symbol, or a word that you want to reinforce and attach the card to a crepe paper necklace. Have the skill holder stand by the door and wear the necklace while the remaining students line up. As each child passes the skill holder, he names or reads what is on the card. Change the skill as desired for a variety of learning opportunities.

Today I was the line leader.
Ask me about my job!

Today I was the door holder.
Ask me about my job!

All About My Job

Use this idea to reinforce the importance of classroom jobs. For each job, program a sheet of paper with statements like the one shown. Make several copies; then cut the statements apart. Store the set for each job in a separate envelope. Each time a student performs a new classroom job, send home a corresponding job strip. Encourage him to talk to his family about his important job.

Ready to Work

Divide a sheet of poster board so it resembles a brick wall. Then make a personalized hard hat for each student (patterns on page 64) and cut out a copy of the job cards on pages 65 and 66. Attach the hook side of a Velcro fastener to each hat and each card. Attach the loop side of two Velcro fasteners to each brick. Then attach a job card to each brick and store the hard hats in a plastic toolbox. For each job, pick a hat from the toolbox and have the student attach her hat to a brick. When it's time to change helpers, remove the hats and pick new ones from the toolbox.

Happy Hands

Use Velcro fasteners to make an adjustable construction paper headband for a special hand-washing helper. Glue to the headband a picture of a handheld soap dispenser and a paper towel. The hand-washing helper wears the headband as he dispenses soap and paper towels to his classmates.

Helper Hound

If your classroom has one helper per day, use this idea to showcase the helper's name. Obtain a stuffed toy dog to be the helper hound and attach a tagboard collar around its neck. For each child, personalize a tagboard dog bone; then store the bones in a plastic dog bowl near the helper hound. Each morning, pick a bone from the bowl to determine the helper of the day. Then use Sticky-Tac to attach the bone to the dog's collar.

Hard Hat Patterns

Use with "Ready to Work" on page 63.

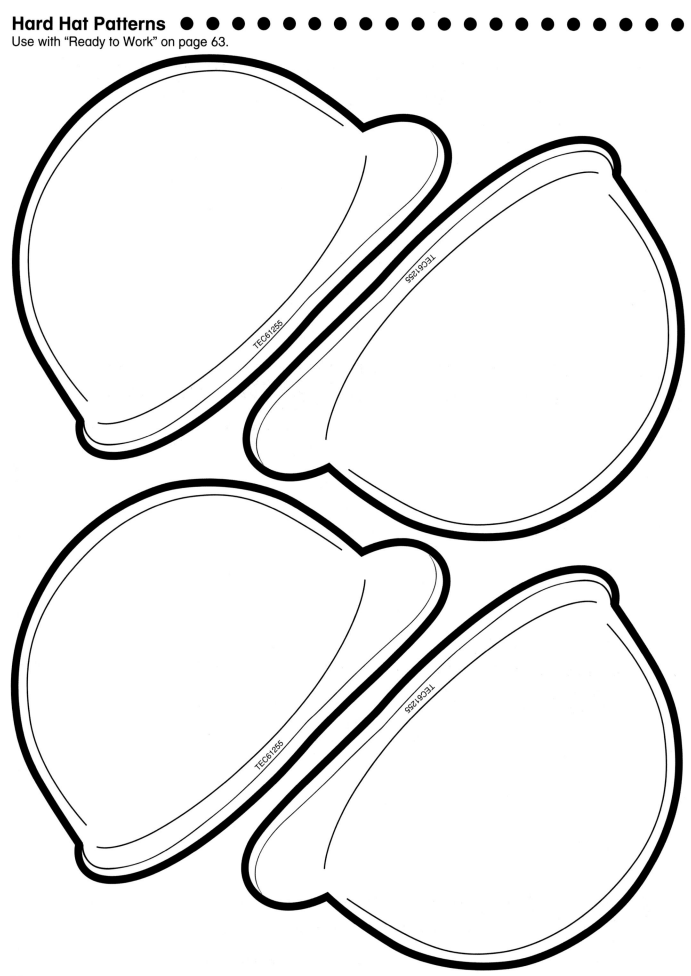

Table Topper
Cleans and sets the tables.
TEC61255

Light Patrol
Turns lights on and off.
TEC61255

Door Holder
Holds door open for the group.
TEC61255

Cubby Keeper
Checks cubbies. Reminds classmates to tidy them if needed.
TEC61255

Weather Watcher
Observes the weather. Helps complete the weather chart.
TEC61255

Library Assistant
Tidies the book area and straightens the books.
TEC61255

EMS Aide

Carries first aid kit to destinations.

TEC61255

Sanitation Helper

Sweeps classroom floor and throws away trash.

TEC61255

Gardener

Checks classroom plants and waters them if needed.

TEC61255

Line Leader

Leads classmates to destinations.

TEC61255

Line Ender

Watches the group and reminds classmates to stay in line.

TEC61255

Supply Helper

CRAYONS
8 LARGE CRAYONS
GLUE

Passes out needed supplies and collects them when finished.

TEC61255

Classroom Library

Color Codes

Color-code your library shelves to keep the books organized. Program a different-colored index card for each category of books. Attach each card to a different shelf. Then attach a corresponding-color sticky dot to each book. Students simply return books to the shelf labeled with the matching color.

Books on File

Here's a simple system that enables you to locate a desired book. Sort your classroom books into categories, such as seasonal, thematic, nursery rhymes, fairy tales, and informational. Label a cardboard divider for each category; then place the dividers and the books in empty computer paper boxes. Make a reference list for each category and attach it to the side of the box. Finding books to read or add to your reading area will be a snap.

Big Book Holder

Use a large flat box, such as one in which poster board is shipped, to store big books. Cut off the box's top flap and half of its front panel. Decorate the box; then use double-sided tape to mount it on a wall or bookcase in your library center.

ELL Students

★ Editor's Pick

Simple Signs

Help your ELL students follow directions with visual cues. Color, cut out, and laminate a copy of the direction cards on page 69. When giving oral directions to complete a task, hold up a matching card or post it on the board. If desired, use the cards to write rebus-style directions on the board.

color

glue

Vocabulary Photo Albums

Create an ELL photo album for use at school and at home. Place in the album labeled photos of classroom and school areas along with snapshots of daily classroom events. Also include labeled clip art or catalog pictures of classroom materials and playground equipment. Refer to the album throughout the day to help youngsters understand upcoming events and connect pictures with words. Support your ELL families by sending the book home and having each student share it with his family.

Picture Prompts

Try using photos to help ELL students follow everyday routines. Take pictures of students engaging in daily activities, such as circle time, lining up, washing hands, eating lunch, and rest time. Mount each photo on a slightly larger card and write the name of the matching activity. Use the cards throughout the day to show your ELL students what they are expected to do.

washing hands

lunchtime

cut

TEC61255

glue

TEC61255

draw

TEC61255

color

TEC61255

read

TEC61255

Taylor

write

TEC61255

Field Trips

First Aid Minikits

Make sure each of your field trip groups has its own emergency kit by filling large resealable plastic bags with first aid items and any other items necessary to accommodate the group. Preparing individual kits assures that each group has the supplies it may need.

Hold On Tight

To help keep students from wandering off during a field trip, cut a length of clothesline for each group. Wrap pieces of colored masking tape around the clothesline at appropriate intervals; then print a child's name on each piece of tape using a permanent marker. Each child has a special place to hold onto during the trip.

Tracking Trips

Keep field trip information handy to help plan next year's outings. Simply fill out a copy of the form on page 71 for each trip. Store the sheets in a binder and then use them as a planning reference.

Field Trip Log

Name of location:
Address:
Phone number:
Contact person:
Cost per child: ___ Per adult:
Bag lunch or snack: ☐ yes ☐ no
Chaperones:

Theme-related trip? ☐ yes ☐ no
If yes, name of theme:
Would you take this trip again? ☐ yes ☐ no
Comments:

Super Simple Classroom Management • ©The Mailbox® Books • TEC61255

See page 72 for a field trip checklist to help with planning and page 73 for reproducible student nametags.

Trip Log

Name of location: _____

Address: _____

Phone number: _____

Contact person: _____

Cost per child: _____   Per adult: _____

Bag lunch or snack: ☐ yes ☐ no

Chaperones: _____   _____

_____   _____

Theme-related trip? ☐ yes ☐ no

If yes, name of theme: _____

Would you take this trip again? ☐ yes ☐ no

Comments: _____

_____

Note to the teacher: Use with "Tracking Trips" on page 70.

Field Trip Checklist

- [ ] Get the address and contact number of your destination; check for hours of operation, cost per child and adult, parking costs, picnic areas, gift shop, and tours.

- [ ] Schedule a rain date.

- [ ] Set up and confirm transportation. If it is a walking trip, plan the safest route.

- [ ] Plan for lunch or snack.

- [ ] Prepare and send home permission slips. Add a note for parents to contact you if they are available to chaperone.

- [ ] Choose chaperones, confirm availability, and record cell phone numbers.

- [ ] Prepare an envelope to collect trip fees and permission slips.

- [ ] Send home reminder notes for students who have not returned permission slips or money.

- [ ] Create groups; assign each group to an adult and prepare nametags (see page 73).

- [ ] Talk with students about the trip, rules, behavior, and safety.

- [ ] Bring an attendance sheet, emergency contact information for each child, first aid kits, extra clothing in case of accidents, and cameras.

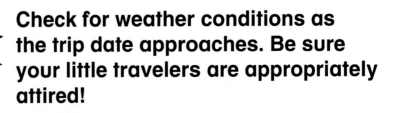

Don't forget to...

Check for weather conditions as the trip date approaches. Be sure your little travelers are appropriately attired!

child

school

TEC61255

child

school

TEC61255

child

school

TEC61255

child

school

TEC61255

child

school

TEC61255

child

school

TEC61255

Health and Hygiene

★ **Editor's Pick**

Achoo!

Remind youngsters to cover their mouths with tissues when they cough or sneeze. If tissues are not available, teach students to sneeze into their upper arms (instead of their hands) to avoid spreading germs to surfaces they touch. Then lead youngsters in singing the song shown, practicing the technique at the end.

(sung to the tune of "If You're Happy and You Know It")

I feel a tickle in my nose. Yes, I do.
I think the tickle's gonna make me say, "Achoo."
Oh, here comes a great big sneeze.
Hurry, pass a tissue, please!
It's too late. I think I'm gonna say, "Achoo!"

Visible Germs

Share with students the importance of using warm water and soap to wash away germs. Sprinkle glitter (germs) on your hands. Then wash your hands in cold water to demonstrate how only some of the germs wash away. Wash your hands again using warm water and soap, demonstrating how to scrub the germs away.

Scrub and Sing

Help little ones scrub their hands for the recommended length of time (15 to 20 seconds) with the help of a favorite song. Display the poster from page 77; then perform the hand-washing procedure shown. When you begin to scrub your lathered hands, sing a song, such as "The Itsy-Bitsy Spider." At the end of the song, rinse your hands clean. Remind youngsters to quietly sing this song each time they wash their hands.

1. Wet your hands with warm water.
2. Add a dab of soap.
3. Scrub your hands, wrists, and between your fingers.
4. Rinse the soap off.
5. Dry your hands with a paper towel.
6. Use the paper towel to turn off the water.

Super Simple Classroom Management •©The Mailbox

See page 75 for a poster that reminds students to cover their mouths when they cough or sneeze.

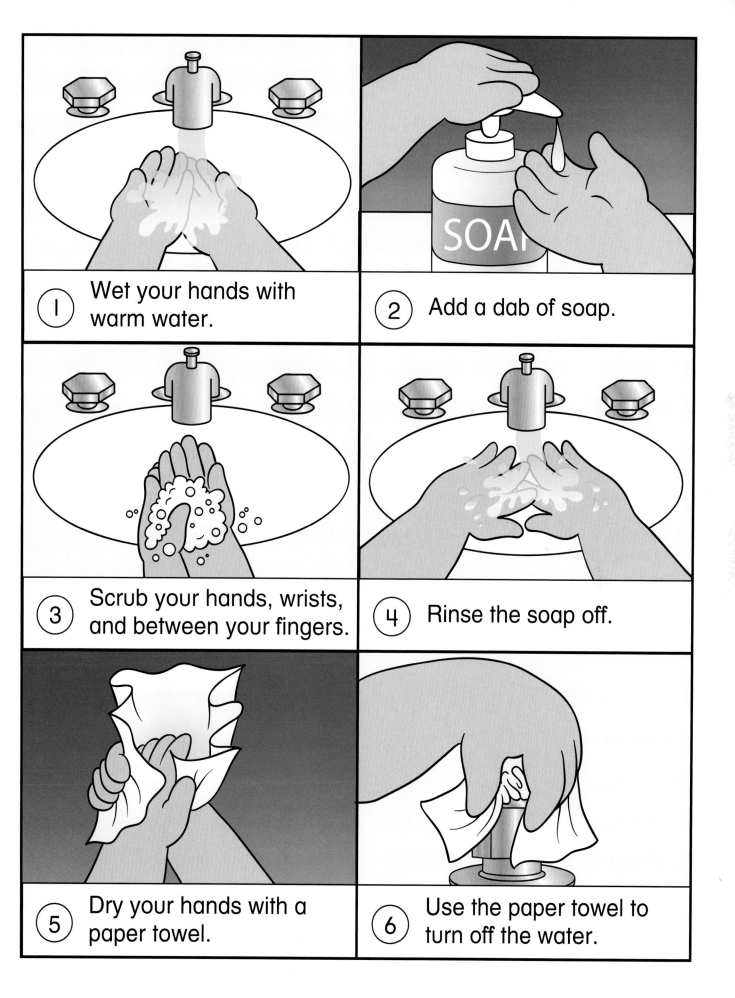

1. Wet your hands with warm water.

2. Add a dab of soap.

3. Scrub your hands, wrists, and between your fingers.

4. Rinse the soap off.

5. Dry your hands with a paper towel.

6. Use the paper towel to turn off the water.

Nap Sacks

To help meet each child's needs during naptime, make a supply of nap sacks. Place inside a small cloth bag activities that can be used quietly and independently, such as a felt background and felt shapes, lacing cards, a small book, and a memo pad and crayons. Provide each child who is unable to sleep or who wakes early with a nap sack to use on his mat while his classmates sleep.

Nap Fairy

Give youngsters incentive to fall asleep. Just before naptime, tell little ones the nap fairy is coming and will leave a special surprise, but she will only come if they are asleep. Once students are asleep, put a sticker on each child's shirt for her to discover upon waking. Periodically change the surprise to maintain youngsters' enthusiasm.

Nighty Night!

Encourage little ones to settle in for naptime with a sleepy-time dramatization. Put on a nightcap and grab a small blanket and a teddy bear. Turn off the lights. Then exaggerate yawns as you walk around the room and help tuck each child in.

See page 80 for naptime awards and page 81 for a sign to display on your door during naptime.

Familiar Voices

Make naptime more relaxing for your little ones by inviting a family member of each child to record himself reading the child's favorite bedtime story. Also ask for a photo of each narrator. To help youngsters settle in for their naps, display a different photo each day and play the corresponding recording.

I am so proud of

_____

for taking a nap today!

teacher's signature

Super Simple Classroom Management • ©The Mailbox® Books • TEC61255

Hip, hip, hooray!

_____ rested today!

teacher's signature

Super Simple Classroom Management • ©The Mailbox® Books • TEC61255

Shhhh!
We Are Resting.

Organizing Student Paperwork

Editor's Pick

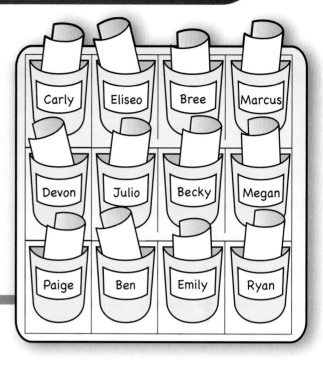

Grab-and-Go Papers

Label each pocket of a shoe organizer with a different child's name. Hang the organizer in an accessible location. File papers to be sent home in the appropriate pockets. At the end of the day, students and parents can easily find the papers they should take home.

Peel and Stick

Save valuable class time with premade name labels. Use a computer to make a supply of personalized self-stick labels for each student. Simply peel and stick the labels to youngsters' projects and paperwork.

All in One Place

Label a hanging file folder for each child and then hang the files in a plastic file crate. (Put a resealable plastic bag in each folder for small items that may get lost in the larger file.) Place the crate in a location accessible to the children. Throughout the day, teachers and students can file items as needed. At the end of the day, each child's papers are easy to find because they are all in one place.

Organizing Teacher Paperwork

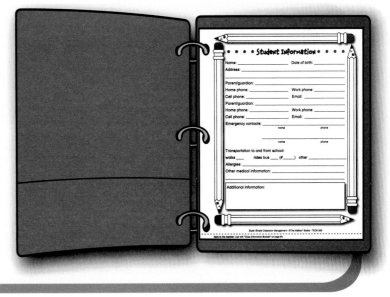

Class Information Booklet

Fill out a copy of the student information form from page 85 for each child. Stack the pages alphabetically between two covers and then hole-punch the pages and covers. Make a booklet using small metal rings to make it easy to add or remove a page. Student information will be at your fingertips in the classroom or on a field trip!

Portable File Boxes

Keep paperwork organized and accessible with this inexpensive, portable filing system. Collect a few empty cereal boxes and cut off the top flaps. Then cover each box with different-colored paper and label it with the name of a task, such as "Do Today," "To Be Filed," or "Things to Go Home." Then place the boxes in a convenient location so you can file papers as needed.

Handy Observations

To manage anecdotal records, prepare a binder with a labeled divider for each student. Place in each child's section a different-colored sheet of paper for each educational area, such as blue for math and yellow for literacy. Jot down observations on sticky notes throughout the day. Date each note and attach it to the corresponding page at a convenient time.

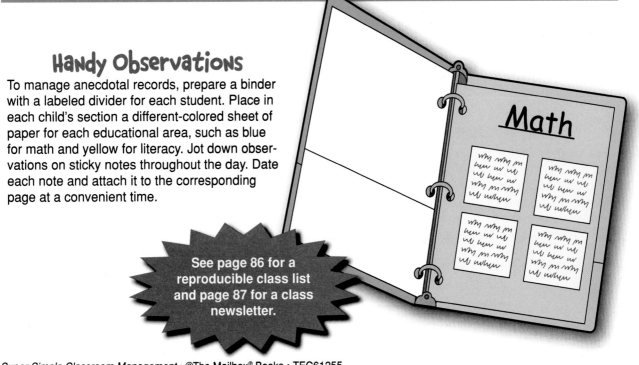

See page 86 for a reproducible class list and page 87 for a class newsletter.

Student Information

Name: _____   Date of birth: _____

Address: _____

_____

Parent/guardian: _____

Home phone: _____   Work phone: _____

Cell phone: _____   Email: _____

Parent/guardian: _____

Home phone: _____   Work phone: _____

Cell phone: _____   Email: _____

Emergency contacts: _____
                              name   phone

                      _____
                              name   phone

Transportation to and from school:

walks ____   rides bus ____ (#_____)   other _____

Allergies: _____

Other medical information: _____

_____

Additional information:

Name								

Class News

From _____

Date _____

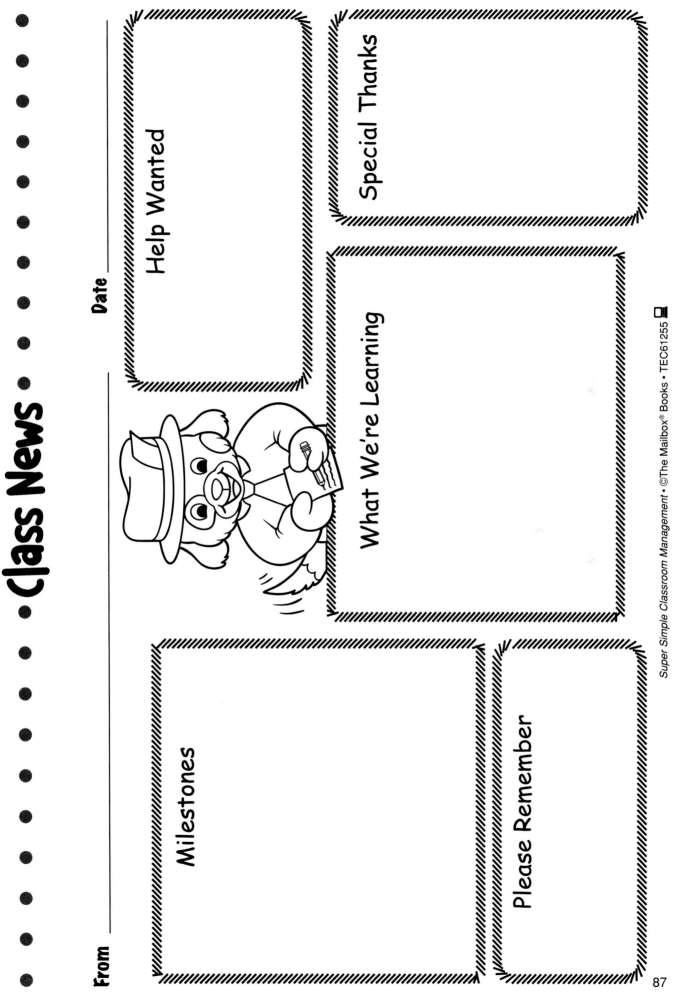

Help Wanted

Special Thanks

What We're Learning

Milestones

Please Remember

Super Simple Classroom Management • ©The Mailbox® Books • TEC61255

Editor's Pick

Paper Bag Portfolios

Make these supersimple portfolios to share student work with parents during conferences. To make a portfolio, have each student decorate a paper grocery bag so it resembles a school bus. Keep the folded portfolios stacked in the classroom and slip work samples into each student's portfolio.

Conference Success

To ensure that your concerns as well as parents' questions and concerns are addressed during a conference, send home a copy of the conference guide on page 91 in advance. Ask each child's family to fill out the guide and bring it to their scheduled conference. In the meantime, fill out a copy of the guide yourself. During the conference, allow time for everyone to share the information they've recorded on their guides.

All About School

Encourage youngsters to share some favorite things about school with their parents. For each student, prepare a booklet containing four pages. Have each child draw one of his favorite things about school on each page. Then have him dictate or write a sentence about each drawing. Share the completed booklet with parents at a conference.

See page 89 for a full-color welcome poster and page 92 for a conference reminder form.

I like singing songs.

Welcome, Parents!

teacher's name

room number

Conference Planning Sheet

Child's name: _____

Conference date: _____

Things that are going well:

-
-
-

Areas of concern:

☐ work habits	☐ respect for others
☐ attitude	☐ gross-motor skills
☐ self-control	☐ fine-motor skills
☐ relations with others	☐ literacy
☐ self-esteem	☐ math
☐ listening skills	☐ other _____

Comments: _____

_____

Other topics to discuss:

-
-
-

Questions:

-
-
-

Super Simple Classroom Management • ©The Mailbox® Books • TEC61255

Note to the teacher: Use with "Conference Success" on page 88.

91

Dear _____,

    I am looking forward to our upcoming conference to discuss _____. We are scheduled to meet on _____ at _____. Please complete the bottom portion of this form and return it to me.

          Sincerely,

_____
teacher's signature

- -

_____   _____
family member's name   child's name

☐ I am able to attend our conference.

☐ I am unable to attend our conference. Please call me at _____ to reschedule.
phone number

Editor's Pick

Communication Station

To help parents stay informed, set up a board and a small table near your classroom door. Post on the board important information such as a class schedule, skills for the week, and upcoming events. On the table, place extra copies of notes that were recently sent home.

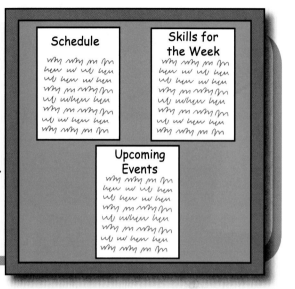

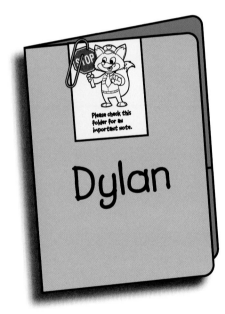

Stop and Check

Here's a quick way to alert parents to an important note in their child's folder. Make several copies of the reminders on page 94 on brightly colored paper and cut them apart. Each time you place an important note in a child's folder, clip a reminder to the front of the folder.

Color Coded

Inform parents that all notes about sending items to school will be copied on a designated color of paper. When parents see a note in that color, they know at a glance that their child needs to bring an item to school.

See page 95 for a parent communication log and page 96 for notes to help you communicate with parents.

Please check this folder for an important note.

TEC61255

Please check this folder for an important note.

TEC61255

Please check this folder for an important note.

TEC61255

Please check this folder for an important note.

TEC61255

Communication Log

Communication Code			
E = email P = phone C = conference N = note			
Date	Who	Type	Reason/Comments

Dear Family,

Please help _____ with

_____ .

Some suggestions are:

_____

_____

_____

Thank you for your help.

_____
teacher's signature

"Dino-mite" News From School

_____ had

_____ a great day because _____

_____

_____ .

_____
teacher's signature

Positive Discipline

To the Treetop!

Place a small reward in each of several plastic eggs; then place the eggs in a basket. Create a display similar to the one shown in an accessible area. Use Sticky-Tac adhesive to attach to the display a personalized bird cutout for each child (patterns on page 98). When a student exhibits exceptional behavior, have him move his bird up the tree. When his bird has reached the top section, invite him to choose an egg and open it to reveal his reward.

Cooling Down

Calm disruptive behavior in a positive way. Assign each student a cool-down spot in an open area of the classroom. If the class becomes restless, encourage students to move to their cool-down spots. Then lead them in simple actions such as taking a deep breath, hopping five times, or performing arm stretches. Continue until the class has calmed down.

Growing Kindness

Use this display to promote kindness among your students. Insert several green craft sticks (stems) into a foam block and place the block in a window box. Set a supply of flower cutouts near the box. When a student is kind to someone, write the date and a sentence about the child's kind act on a flower. Then help the student tape the flower to a stem.

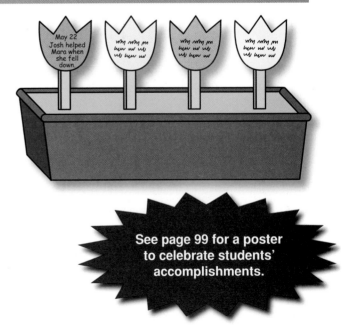

See page 99 for a poster to celebrate students' accomplishments.

Super Simple Classroom Management • ©The Mailbox® Books • TEC61255

Hip, Hip, Hooray

for

_____

name(s)

because _____

_____

_____ .

Attach photo here.

Planning for a Substitute

A Sweet Thank-You

Show your appreciation for a substitute by attaching a small treat to a copy of the rhyme at the top of page 102. Have a student or your classroom aide present the treat to the substitute at the end of the day.

A day like this is always fun
With a substitute so sweet.
Our class thinks having a sub like you
Is pretty hard to beat!

Candy

Extra Time

Help a substitute keep youngsters on task all day. Complete the form on page 103 and place any necessary materials in a box labeled "Substitute Extras." Leave the form with your lesson plans and let the substitute know that if she has extra time she should choose something from the list to do with students.

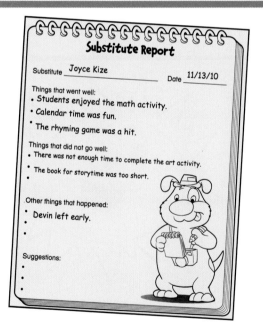

Substitute Report

Substitute __Joyce Kize__   Date __11/13/10__

Things that went well:
• Students enjoyed the math activity.
• Calendar time was fun.
• The rhyming game was a hit.

Things that did not go well:
• There was not enough time to complete the art activity.
• The book for storytime was too short.

Other things that happened:
• Devin left early.
•
•

Suggestions:
•
•
•

Teacher Notes

Encourage a substitute to communicate information about her day with this easy-to-complete form. Attach a copy of the form on page 104 to your plans and ask the substitute to complete the form at the end of the day.

In One Place

A substitute will have necessary materials at her fingertips with this idea. Place in a tub or basket a copy of the lesson plans along with the materials needed to execute the plans. This ensures that the substitute will have everything she needs for a successful day.

See page 102 for a half-page note that a substitute can share with students and page 105 for a form to use when creating your substitute plans.

A day like this is always fun
With a substitute so sweet.
Our class thinks having a sub like you
Is pretty hard to beat!

Super Simple Classroom Management • ©The Mailbox® Books • TEC61255

Note to the teacher: Use with "A Sweet Thank-You" on page 101.

Substitute: Please read this letter aloud to students at the start of the day. At the end of the day, write positive comments you would like to share with me on the attached class list. Thank you!

An Invitation to Shine!

Dear boys and girls,

I'm sorry that I won't see you today. I will miss out on all the fun! Please have your substitute teacher write to tell me all the good things you did for him/her and for your friends today. I know you will have a wonderful day because you are a great class!

_____
teacher's signature

Super Simple Classroom Management • ©The Mailbox® Books • TEC61255

Note to the teacher: Sign a copy of the letter and staple it atop a class list that includes space for a brief comment beside each child's name. Place the letter and the list with other information you leave for your substitute.

Got Extra Time?

Favorite Books	Favorite Games

Favorite Songs and Poems	Other Activities

Substitute Report

Substitute _____   Date _____

Things that went well:

-
-
-

Things that did not go well:

-
-
-

Other things that happened:

-
-
-

Suggestions:

-
-
-

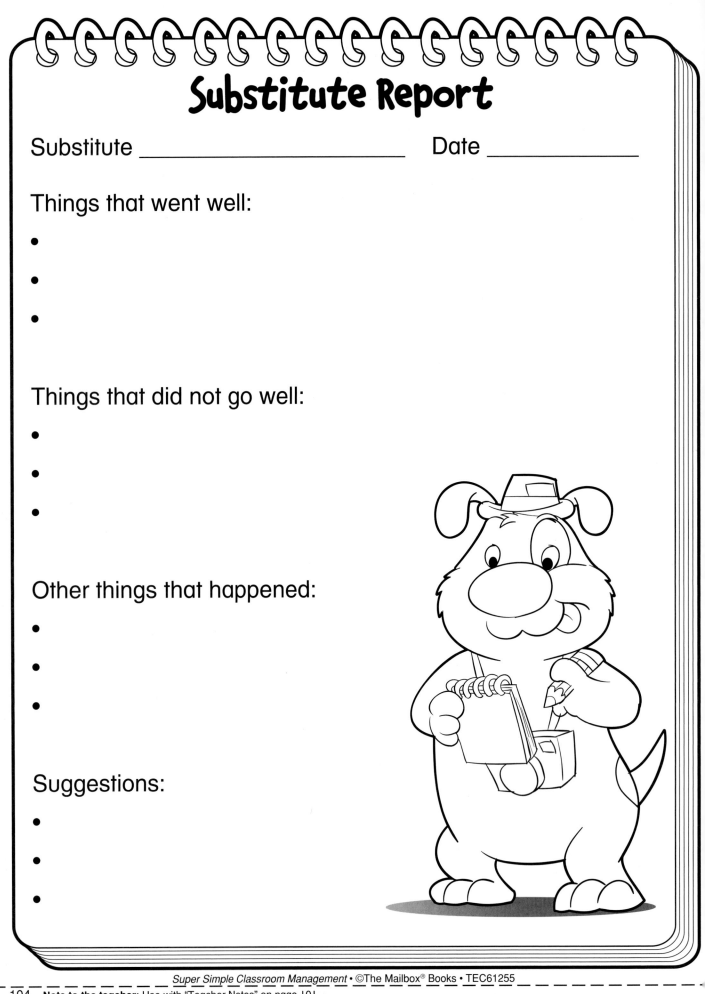

Super Simple Classroom Management • ©The Mailbox® Books • TEC61255

104   **Note to the teacher:** Use with "Teacher Notes" on page 101.

Substitute Plans

Time	Activity	Description	Materials

Smooth Transitions

Get Them Ready

To find out quickly who is ready for the next task, ask, "All set?" and snap your fingers twice. Children who are ready respond, "You bet!" while the others say, "Not yet." If necessary, wait a few moments and repeat the question. This upbeat exchange prompts students to get ready without making them feel anxious.

Try Stuffed Toys

Keep a collection of stuffed animals handy. When you call students to the rug for storytime, ask a student helper to observe her classmates and choose several who move to the area promptly and quietly. Then have her present each of these students with a stuffed toy to hold while the story is being read.

Work Out the Wiggles

If you have an active child who needs to work out extra energy during transitions, tape a tagboard square on the floor in a secluded area. If the child demonstrates a need to use stored energy, have him visit the square and jump there until he's ready to stop or you're ready for him to rejoin the group.

Jingle and Shake

When you want youngsters to move from one activity to the next, pull out a set of keys and give them a shake to get everyone's attention. Then recite the chant shown, inserting your next activity in the last line, to get children to shift gears.

Now it's time to turn the key.
Start your car and drive with me!
Where to next? Do you know?
It's time to [wash our hands]. Let's go!

Welcoming New Students

Editor's Pick

A Warm Welcome

Extend a warm welcome to a student who joins your class during the year by mailing her a completed copy of the welcome card from page 108. Along with the card, send a class photo and a personal welcome note signed by each student.

Welcome,
Rebecca **!**
student's name
I'm so happy you're joining my class!

Ms. Parker
teacher's signature

Super Simple Classroom Management • ©The Mailbox® Books • TEC61255

Welcome Buddies

During a new student's first week in your class, select a different volunteer each day to be a welcome buddy. Cut out copies of the student badges on page 108 and personalize the buttons for each student to wear. Discuss with the welcome buddy ways he can help the new student, such as guide her through the daily routine and help her locate things in the classroom.

We're All Smiles That You Joined Our Class!

Smiles

We have fun learning in our class!

Lexi

Our

We're All Smiles!

To make a class welcome book, give each child a white paper circle. Encourage her to write or dictate words for you to write to welcome a new student to your class. Next, have her illustrate the page. Bind the pages together between two covers; then draw a happy face on the front cover and title the book as shown. Read the book during circle time. Finally, send it home with the new student to share with his family.

New Student Welcome Card ● ● ● ● ● ● ● ● ● ● ● ● ● ● ● ● ● ●
Use with "A Warm Welcome" on page 107.

Welcome, ____!

student's name

I'm so happy you're joining my class!

____
teacher's signature

Super Simple Classroom Management • ©The Mailbox® Books • TEC61255

Student Badges ● ● ● ● ● ● ● ● ● ● ● ● ● ● ● ● ● ●
Use with "Welcome Buddies" on page 107.

Meet my new buddy, ____!

TEC61255

Welcome Buddy's Badge

Hi! I'm ____'s new buddy!

TEC61255

New Student's Badge

At the End of the Year

Kindergarten Certificate

Presented to

Liam Murphy

for participation in kindergarten at

Brier Creek Elementary

Mrs. Troxler
teacher

June 4, 2010
date

Preschool Certificate

Presented to

Emma Robertson

for completion of preschool at

First-Step Preschool

Jena Salmons
teacher

June 4, 2010
date

What a Great Year!

Memories and Expectations

This class book is a fun way to end one school year and also to begin a new one. On a sheet of paper, have each student draw a favorite activity from the school year. Then have him write or dictate a sentence about his drawing. Bind the completed pages into a book. After sharing the book with your class, store it in an accessible location. On the first day of the next school year, read the book to your new class to let them know about the upcoming year.

The trip to the farm was fun.

Class Projects

Invite each student to take home a memory of the school year. To begin, display class books and other whole-group projects made during the year. Personalize a paper strip for each child and place the strips in a basket. Choose a strip and read the child's name and have her choose a book or project to keep as a memento. Continue until each student has chosen a keepsake.

Memory Toss

Youngsters use a colorful beach ball to share memories of the school year. Designate a question related to the school year for each color on a beach ball. Sit with students in a circle and roll the ball to a student. Have the child catch the ball and name a color that one of his hands is touching. Then ask him the corresponding question. After he answers the question, have him roll the ball to a classmate. Continue until each child has had a turn.

What is the funniest thing that happened this year?

Preschool Certificate

Presented to

for completion of preschool at

teacher

date

Kindergarten Certificate

Presented to

_____

for participation in kindergarten at

_____

_____
teacher

_____
date